NEO SKILLS OF MARKETING

ZERO PAIN MARKETING STRATEGIES FOR NON-TECHIE ENTREPRENEURS

SUMESH M NAIR

Copyright © Sumesh M Nair
All Rights Reserved.

ISBN 978-1-63920-625-4

This book has been published with all efforts taken to make the material error-free after the consent of the author. However, the author and the publisher do not assume and hereby disclaim any liability to any party for any loss, damage, or disruption caused by errors or omissions, whether such errors or omissions result from negligence, accident, or any other cause.

While every effort has been made to avoid any mistake or omission, this publication is being sold on the condition and understanding that neither the author nor the publishers or printers would be liable in any manner to any person by reason of any mistake or omission in this publication or for any action taken or omitted to be taken or advice rendered or accepted on the basis of this work. For any defect in printing or binding the publishers will be liable only to replace the defective copy by another copy of this work then available.

To all Non-Techie Entrepreneurs & Small Business Owners

Contents

Preface	vii
1. 7 Simple Yet Powerful Proven Ways To Make $10,000 From Your Business Every Month	1
2. Neo Skills Of Marketing	3
3. Principle Of Neo Skills Marketing	5

THE FOCUS SKILLS

4. Skill #1 Psychology	9
5. Skill #2 Creativity	12
6. Skill #3 Strategy	14

THE REFINE SKILLS

7. Skill #4 Metrics	19
8. Skill #5 Optimize	22

THE SCALE SKILLS

9. Skill #6 Systems	27
10. Skill #7 Execution	29
11. Conclusion	31
Claim Your $499 Worth 5 Days 1 Hour Neo Skills Workshop For Just $99	33

Preface

7 Simple Yet Powerful Proven Ways to make $10,000 from your Business in the next 30 Days

Obtaining $10,000 every month is one of the greatest feelings you can experience as a small business owner. There is simply nothing else like it. That's because when you obtain $10,000 every month, you get to enjoy leisure time with your family, have peace of mind as you can generate secure and adequate income to meet the needs of your family and your employees, can run the business ethically and fairly, can think about expanding your business without having any mortgages etc.

However, there are many obstacles you have to overcome before you can get there. Not only do you have to overcome cash flow issues, higher expenses, pending mortgages – but you also have to overcome your Sales issues, which can be the most difficult challenge of all. All of this can leave you falling well short of the mark and stop you from ever achieving your Millionaire dream (if you have).

Fortunately, though, obtaining monthly $10,000 doesn't have to be as challenging as you think. Far from it, in fact. Simply by implementing the right tried-and-tested techniques, you can achieve the desired monthly outcome without experiencing any common frustrations.

How would we know?

Because, at Gaude Business Solutions, we're experts at

helping café's/restaurants, boutiques, tour operators, start-ups, spa and saloons, institutes, home maintenance companies, trainers etc. achieve their desired outcomes in less than 6 months. Over the past 14 years, we've helped 380+ clients achieve their desired outcome without the years of hard work and trial and error most people usually have to suffer through.

I've written this book to share some of the powerful industry secrets that I've accumulated during my time in the IT industry. The information you're about to read will help you achieve your monthly $10000 while making sure you avoid the common mistakes and conventional marketing strategies.

You're about to discover:

- 7 Simple Yet Powerful Proven Ways to Make $10,000 from your Business in the Next 30 Days

- 7 insider secrets that can help you achieve monthly $10,000 in as little as 4weeks!

- The TRUTH about small business owners and why you like business owners usually fail at achieving your desired outcome

By the time you've finished ready, you'll have all the information you need to kick start your journey to success and achieve $10,000 monthly revenue.

Let's get started!

CHAPTER ONE

7 Simple Yet Powerful Proven Ways to make $10,000 from your Business Every Month

Some days, $10,000 monthly revenue from your business might seem like a faraway dream. But, if you implement the right strategies, you can get there far sooner than you think. I've outlined 7 simple, tried-and-tested techniques you can use to achieve your monthly $10,000 goal. This technique is termed as "Neo Skills of Marketing" and you should apply "Neo Skills" every time to your marketing then, you can even achieve your Millionaire goal within a year itself. And one day, you will realize the fact that this is the only ZERO PAIN Marketing Strategy used by World's fastest-growing entrepreneurs.

Every single Entrepreneur, including YOU, has the potential to become a Millionaire Marketer or Millionaire Business Owner and scale your business to Million Dollar Revenue in less than a year's time. But you need to master the skills that separate you from them.

I took almost 6 years to master those skills and the required tools, and it costs me around half a million dollar to become an expert in such skills. With those skills, I am in my Agency helping hundreds of clients every month to achieve their desired goals.

And with this book, my wholehearted promise to you is to help you discover those skills.

CHAPTER TWO

NEO SKILLS OF MARKETING

If you notice, many Entrepreneurs struggle with their marketing because they are running after the latest and the greatest marketing "Strategy" in their industry. And, that's the reason they burn their money on advertisements.

NEO SKILLS OF MARKETING not only focusing on the Strategy. Here are the 7 pillars of Neo Skills Marketing. All these 7 skills are interconnected. Mostly Neo Skills are applying to Online Marketing, which is the future that you may know.

1. *Psychology*
2. *Creativity*
3. *Strategy*
4. *Metrics*
5. *Optimize*
6. *Systems*
7. *Execution*

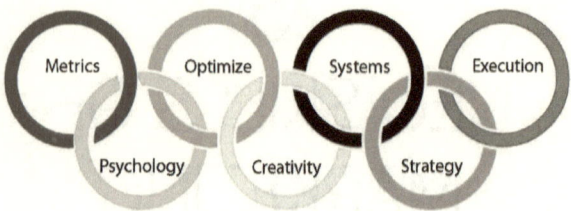

7 Skills of Neo Skills Marketing

CHAPTER THREE

Principle of Neo Skills Marketing

We need to understand the Buyer first.

> "*Without the skills of understanding buyer "Psychology" and communicating a message with "Creativity", Marketing "Strategy" won't work.*"

So as per our Neo Skills principle, your focus should be in this order: ***Psychology, Creativity, and Strategy***. I'll be covering everything about the 7 skills in the next chapter.

Once you launch your Online Marketing Campaigns based on this strategy and start getting results, you need to make them consistent and predictable.

So, the next skill set is refining the campaigns by properly tracking "***Metrics***" and "***Optimize***" the campaigns till you have a winning campaign that can be scaled.

Once you refined it properly, it can be automated or outsourced; you create "***Systems***" and "***Execute***" them to scale your campaigns to Million Dollars or more.

Don't worry if any of the above doesn't make sense to you right now; it will make all the sense when you finish reading this book.

THE FOCUS SKILLS

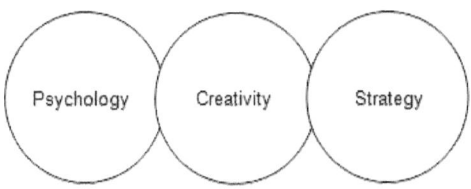

CHAPTER FOUR

SKILL #1 PSYCHOLOGY

If you're serious about achieving $10,000 monthly revenue from your business, one of the first things you absolutely must do is to understand "Psychology" of your Buyer.

All of your competitors are looking for new Sales/Business Leads, am I right?

So how to attract new leads to your business?

You need to have a "**Leads Magnet**". You know the meaning of magnet;it can attract, right?

So a "Leads Magnet" also does the same, it will attract "Leads" to your business.

Interesting?

HOW TO MAKE LEADS MAGNET OF YOUR BUSINESS?

In order to make a Leads Magnet, you should understand

the 3 Focus Skills which I said earlier: Psychology, Creativity & Strategy.

Let me explain to you what PSYCHOLOGY in Business means?

WHY PEOPLE BUY FROM YOU?

If you understand the Psychology behind this question: WHY PEOPLE BUY FROM YOU, you are miles ahead of your competitors. Let me show you this with my ad copy below.

Around 3700 people from different countries have joined so far for my 5 Days WhatsApp Training Workshop of Neo Skills, and that too within a short time of 30 days.

Why did so many people join this workshop in a short time?

It's because they wanted to move from "Procrastination" to "Productivity".

I mean, all the products we buy are because we want to stop procrastinating our unproductivity with our current habits/things and become more productive with new skills, habits/things.

So you should put your foot on the shoes of a Marketer and then find what level of new "Productivity" people are buying now in your market with their hard-earned money, then only you will be able to understand their Psychological buying patterns.

It's not rocket science.

Just Google your industry's Top 10 products/services and then browse through all their marketing materials. Those are the Leads Magnet of your competitors. Now you have to draft your own Leads Magnet with good Creativity.

CHAPTER FIVE

SKILL #2 CREATIVITY

As well as Psychology, you also need to understand the second pillar of Neo Skills: "Creativity", if you're ever going to achieve your monthly revenue goal. This is really powerful because it is communicating with your Prospects. I would like to call this the FACE of your Lead Magnet.

So How to make the Creativity of your Product/Services?

Creativity means the way you are communicating about your products/services to your prospects. It can sometimes be stories or images, or videos.

Make sure that in all your Creativity, there should be three things:

- **Pain areas of your Prospects**
- **Dreams & Desires / Outcome & Result of your Prospects**
- **How have other people moved from their pain areas to their desired output with your product/solution**

Pain areas of prospects mean you should able to find out the fears and frustrations your prospects are facing right now.

Also, you should think about the dreams and desires of your prospects, which your competitors do not acknowledge.

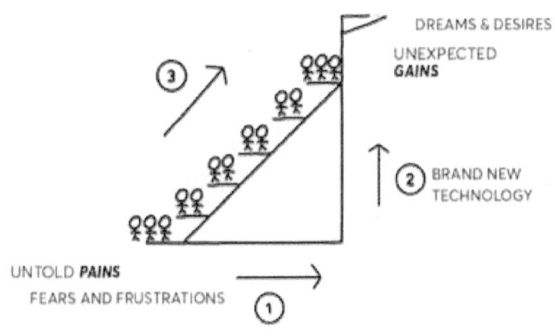

CHAPTER SIX

SKILL #3 STRATEGY

If you look at any Online Marketing or Digital Marketing Strategies, it's all talking about 3 Elements

- Traffic
- Value
- Offer

Traffic means sending prospects from different sources like Facebook, Google, YouTube, messenger, WhatsApp,etc., to your website.

Value means your website or landing pages or your ad content or emails/newsletter

Do you know all your marketing problems lie on one thing, and you know what that is?

It is "YOU TRY TO MAKE AN OFFER BEFORE YOU CREATE VALUE"

You should create a tangible value for your prospect before you make an actual offer.

For example, in my case, I always try to give my prospects my ebook or High Conversion web template for a very small fee or sometimes as freebies. When they experience its result, they will eitherJoin my 5 Days Training Workshop or hire my agency service. I gave them a tangible result with my value, and they understood I can help them achieve their dreams and desired outcomes by overcoming their challenges with my years of experience, skills, and knowledge.

You need to have this kind of strategy in your business, and it will help you start long term relationship with your potential clients.

THE REFINE SKILLS

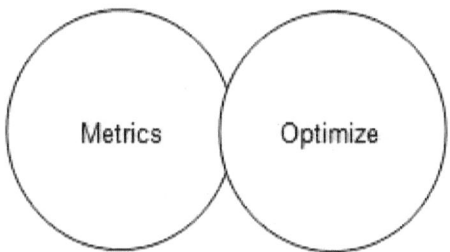

CHAPTER SEVEN

SKILL #4 METRICS

People usually don't track metrics in their Marketing, they think that it's too technical and complicated. Hence, I was thinking about creating new metrics by analyzing all the existing successful metrics, which perhaps even a non-techie entrepreneur can use to track their marketing system. It took many years for me to find out these metrics, and then I did thousands of trials& tests to see how it is working. Finally, I added it to our "Neo Skills".

With Neo Skills Marketing, all you need to scale your business from Zero to a Million Dollar or more is to measure just 2 metrics of 2 funnels.

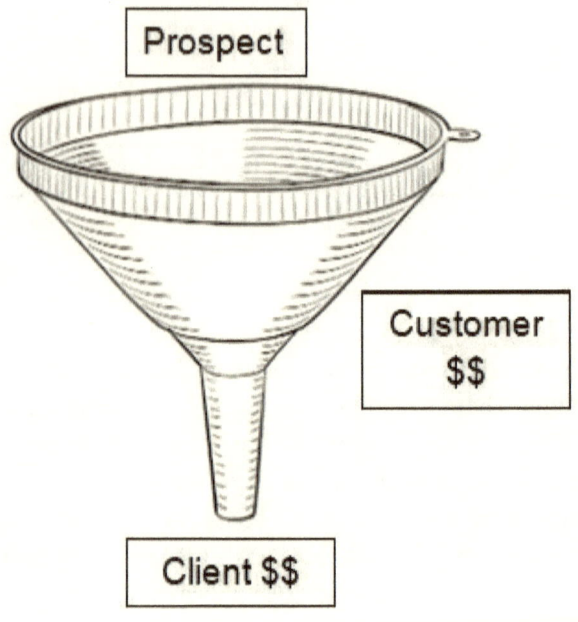

Almost 90% of the business owners are building their Sales funnel with 1 metric, but here I want to show you what difference Neo Skills can make - if you create your 2 Sales Funnels with 2 metrics:

1. Customer Funnel
2. Client Funnel

You need to see your entire Marketing strategy with 2 Funnels. If so, you can convert your Prospect to Customer (a First time Buyer with Low Ticket Sales), and then later, you Convert your Customers to Clients (Repeat Buyers probably with High Ticket Sales).

If you want to learn more about this, you can join my 5 Days 1-hour training workshop on "Neo Skills of Marketing" any time from my website www.learnneoskills.com.

CHAPTER EIGHT

SKILL #5 OPTIMIZE

Many people don't know about this one skill, "Optimize", which is crazy because we think it's an absolute MUST-DO when it comes to achieving your Millionaire Goal.

It would be best if you did many optimizations on your advertisement and its costs, otherwise, you will burn your fingers for ads.

Earlier, you were trying to put ads of your products or services on many platforms to get end clients, but now you learned a two-step funnel metrics, and thereby, you only need to look for the Customer Acquisition Cost. For example, if you want to sell a $550 offer, you need to make sure that the cost doesn't exceed $550 to acquire a customer.

You need to look into joining ventures, referral partners & affiliates to acquire customers at a much lesser cost so that you can achieve break-even with the Customer Funnel itself.

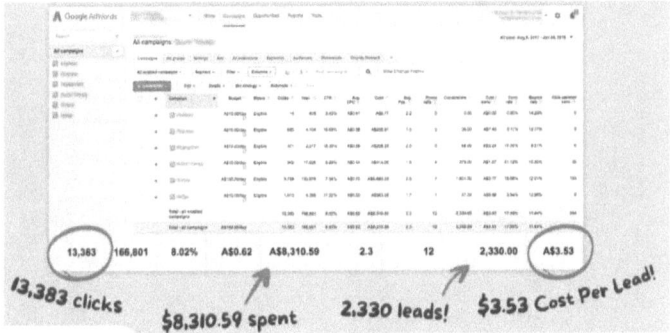

Please see one of my client's ad spend on Google. Once you master Neo Skills, you will see this kind of results for sure, but you need to have time, patience, and money.

THE SCALE SKILLS

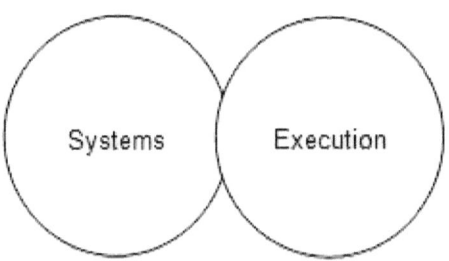

CHAPTER NINE

SKILL #6 SYSTEMS

You need to build Systems if you want to scale your business faster without waiting more time.

Don't need to be scared with the term "Systems".

For example, you can implement the following systems by yourself to scale your business faster:

- MARKETING SYSTEM
- REFERRAL SYSTEM
- CASE STUDY SYSTEM
- FOLLOW UP SYSTEM
- SALES SYSTEM

    - *On Marketing System, you can start with creating 2 videos/images per week*
    - *A Referral System can be giving away a digital product when they refer 4 people to your customer funnel*
    - *A Case Study system could be just scheduling two successful clients for the zoom call every week, record it and show it in your Values*

- *Follow Up System can be sending the links of your recent Case Studies to your Customers who didn't become your clients*
- *Sales system could offer your first freebies or very less price product or services (Lead Magnet pitch)*

CHAPTER TEN

SKILL #7 EXECUTION

Here comes the final Skill of Neo Skills.

Do you know how to execute all the systems without getting overwhelmed?

It's very simple, but only if you practice.

All you have to do is divide each system into doable daily tasks and work on them every day.

For example: if you want to create 2 videos in your Marketing System, you can create a weekly execution schedule like this:

Day 1: Create Script/Story Board of 1st Video

Day 2: Record Video

Day 3: Create Script/Story Board of 2nd Video

Day 4: Record Video

Day 5: Launch Video Ads

This is an example of an actionable schedule of Neo Skills. You can do all the Systems by yourself, or you can hire an agency to do it for you.

CHAPTER ELEVEN

Conclusion

That's the Neo Skills behind 7 Simple Yet Powerful Proven Ways to Make $10,000 from your Business every month. It has helped thousands of my students and around 380 clients achieve their Level Zero goalà Level Millionaire. I hope it does the same for you as well.

Get your exclusive claim bonus for reading this book by flipping to on next page.

Claim Your $499 Worth 5 Days 1 Hour Neo Skills Workshop For Just $99

Thank you for taking the time to read this Book – I hope you've found the information helpful and can use what you've learned to reach even your Millionaire Dream.

If you're truly serious about achieving your monthly $10,000 revenue business, then I have excellent news exclusively for you. We're offering you a 5 Days 1 hour workshop of Neo Skills for an exclusive OFFER for a limited time only. You will be trained Step-by-Step process to launch your online marketing campaign to achieve your monthly $10,000 goal.

We'll discuss your current situation during our session, what your goals are, and how we can help you achieve them using our proven system.

We'll also cover a stack of valuable information together, including...

How you can achieve half a million business in 6 months, what you should never do when trying to achieve monthly $10,000 goal, and how to avoid all the most common mistakes that small business owners make every time which sabotages their success.

If you want to learn these skills from any other institute or expert, it may cost you thousands of dollars, and also you may need to spend 1 or 2 years to learn everything. My 5 Days 1-hour Training Workshop is a proven and

CLAIM YOUR $499 WORTH 5 DAYS 1 HOUR NEO SKILLS WORKSHOP FOR JUST $99

predictable ZERO PAIN Marketing workshop for non-techie entrepreneurs. You will be launching your Successful Funnel by yourself on the 5thDay of our Workshop.

I am going to teach you the following things step-by-step:

Day #1 – Overview of Neo Skills, Most Needed Tools & Knowledge

Day #2 - Creating Your Lead Magnet

Day #3 - Building Your Lead Squeeze Funnel

Day #4 - Writing Your Follow-Up Funnel Sequence

Day #5 - Launching Your Funnel and Generating Your First Leads!

To claim your OFFER FEE of **$99**, or find out more information about this limited-time offer, all you have to do is click the link- http://www.learnneoskills.com/

GOOD LUCK

www.ingramcontent.com/pod-product-compliance
Lightning Source LLC
Chambersburg PA
CBHW020949180526
45163CB00006B/2370